Stones
WILL
Shout

HELEN E. HERR

Helen E. Herr

"splashing free"

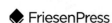 FriesenPress

Suite 300 - 990 Fort St
Victoria, BC, V8V 3K2
Canada

www.friesenpress.com

ISBN
978-1-5255-4742-3 (Hardcover)
978-1-5255-4743-0 (Paperback)
978-1-5255-4744-7 (eBook)

1. POETRY

Distributed to the trade by The Ingram Book Company

for my family and all the readers
who love a good story

Table of Contents

in memory of our two sons

Kirby James Herr (1965 – 2012)
Ronald Cecil Meetoos (1964 – 2016)

Acknowledgements

I have enjoyed the unique opportunity to have many
authors journey with me in my writing. Established
writers in our family, Shelley A. Leedahl and Taylor
Leedahl, have always been available to listen, support
and edit my poems over the years. My husband, Jim,
for listening to my readings day and night. Thank you
to Lonnie Mason, Donna Frandsen and Wendy Thompson
for their early critiques. I appreciate the Saskatchewan Writers' Guild
and the Blue Sky Writers' support. Special thanks to FriesenPress
for their expertise and publication. Taylor, thanks for writing the
note for the back cover.

I have attended SWG workshops and retreats with Janice
Dick, Shelley A. Leedahl, Brenda Baker, Leona Theis,
Lynda Monahan and Barbara Langhorst. Thanks to the
Writers-in-Residence: John Barton, Anne Simpson,
Rosemary Nixon and Katherine Lawrence.

A special thanks to friends and strangers who come
to my readings or have purchased my first book of poetry.
I hope my thoughts and words enhance your life journey.
Blessings to you from Helen.

Preface
by Helen E. Herr

more than stones

I talk to stones—not loose pebbles scattered on the ground
but soapstones found deep below the earth around the world.
When I carve groves and curves in my stones, poetic lines
take shape. I ask: Is this who I am? What about my future?

Each stone differs in colour and density. My poems also vary;
some are sunny, others dark. Regardless of our age, race,
or circumstance, I believe we all have similar feelings.

Everyone has a unique story. My story is crying out to be heard.
As you open each page, listen for your own story.

The title **Stones Will Shout** refers to Luke19:39-40 NRSV

> *I tell you, if these were silent,*
> *the stones would shout out.*

Helen E. Herr

quiet until the diamond
drill sends you quivering
into my hands—
I uncover your heart
open two black eyes

in the beginning

I close my eyes
the sun's bright—
I prefer the dark.

You see, I came into the world too soon.
Premature, only two pounds.
Born at home in Eston, Saskatchewan.
My dad said:
        I held you in the palm of my hand.
Together with my uncle, they built an incubator
from an apple box, heated it with a light bulb.

My mother thought I wouldn't survive,
        (she'd already lost two babies at birth)
so she over-protected me.

Now, as a senior, I share my story with you.
Our experiences will be different, but perhaps
we may meet along the way.

Helen E. Herr

smooth wet stones

I am almost eight when we move
to Regina. I can hear my mother:

> *Don t leave the yard alone, watch*
> *for traffic. Dad will drive you to school,*
> *slow down on our stairs.*

A two-year-old boy lives next door.
We share the same back lawn.
One Saturday afternoon, Mom sees
me put my arms around the child.
She runs to get her camera.
I pose again but never tell her
I pick stones out of his mouth
every day.

coal dust

I'm scared of our basement!
Sometimes it floods.
The night is black when the furnace
pipes bang and shake.

I hold a flashlight tight
as I sneak into the basement.
Pretend I'm a ghost crouching
in the coal bin under the stairs.

I listen—sounds like a bird is caught.
Perhaps he needs a friend.
I call him "Honker".
Mom stomps down.
> *What are you doing down here?*
> *Get up stairs, now!*
She doesn't believe there's a bird hiding
in the pipes.
> *Don't ever come down here again!*

When everyone sleeps, I open the door
a crack and talk to Honker. He hears
my voice, becomes quiet.

spinning!

The moon covers my ears.
I don't want to hear my mother's voice
rise as she scrapes, chips and fills
cracks in the living room hardwood
floor.

I hate it when my parents shout.
The dishes crash and Dad slams
the front door, again.

I know the grout will be dry in the morning.
I slip on my red and white polka dot socks,
creep downstairs and touch the finished floor—
            smooth as ice.

I twirl on one leg around and around,
don't even get one sliver in my foot.

before the cross

I begin piano lessons in Regina, eight years old.
Since music is taught at the convent
on Thirteenth Avenue and we live close by,
a Catholic Sister will be my teacher.

The Sisters, in their long black habits, swish
through dim-lit corridors as they scurry towards
the chapel. I hide in doorways. Afraid I'll be grabbed,
dragged before the cross where Jesus hangs—
his blood dripping on my robin's-egg blue dress,
the one that matches my eyes.

I never tell my parents I skip lessons.
After two weeks, Sister phones: *Is Helen sick?*

My next piano lesson is in Darke Hall
on College Avenue. The basement is brighter
but also mysterious.
          (doors open and close, open-close)
to teachers' voices, sharp as high C.

initiation

Grade four, my parents allow me to join
friends every Wednesday after school
at the Regina roller-skating rink.
We're not sure about boys, so the girls
link arms, swing to the "The Blue Danube".
Sometimes, we fall in the corners.

Most often we sit on benches
in the girls' dressing room, pass cigarettes
we've snuck from older siblings or parents.
            (they'll never know)
One puff (cough, cough, cough)
as we learn to blow perfect smoke rings—
Marilyn Munroe-style.

Everything changes the day Judie's dad
knocks on the door, gazes through the haze.
Calls Judie home.

Five days later, we're told her mother died.
Next Wednesday, we pass cigarettes in silence—
blow perfect smoke rings, just for Judie.

gypsy and her fans

While waiting for my Honda's oil change,
I thumb the *Saskatoon Home* magazine,
summer, 2016, page fifty-nine:

> *The Saskatoon Exhibition: After WWII,*
> *attendance increased with the arrival*
> *of dancer Gypsy Rose Lee.*

When she comes to Regina, I'm thirteen,
sitting under a huge tent with my parents. It seems odd
to be the only child, front row and center,
surrounded by men shouting: *More, more!*
Line dancers' kick high in seamless rows
of floating feathers and flashing lights.

The highlight is the finale: Gypsy Rose at the top
of a spiralling staircase, spreads her feathered fans,
arms wide for total exposure. The crowd goes wild!

> My mother tells me later:
> *Gypsy Rose was wearing three pasties.*
> *Not totally naked.*

It's the only sex education my parents ever gave me.

Helen E. Herr

speaking tongues

I write because it's in my genes,
four generations of women.

When words whisper in the night,
I become a tree married to the soil.

> *cows moon-eye me*
> *through the fence—*
> *writing poetry*
> *cross-legged*
> *in the ditch[*]*

On days when verses stutter
or repeat themselves, I grow
into a snap-dragon or screeching
tongues of magpies on a compost,
or clothes flapping in the wind.

---

[*]   *Gusts No11, Spring/summer 2010, p.22*

put on your hiking boots

Shelley A. Leedahl, our daughter,
a prolific writer who creates poetry,
prose and essays, often references
her world travels:

> Mazatlan waters on a boogie board
> among jellyfish, or Bali on a motorcycle
> dodging traffic and dogs.

Shelley lives in British Columbia.
The salt air brushes her hair as she
runs twenty kilometres on Ladysmiths'
winding trails. Her freezer is full
of blackberries from prickly bushes
locals avoid.

making waves

Taylor, I remember your fourth year
when I lifted you from the pool, long
hair dripping as we walk hand-in-hand
to your home for cookies and milk.

Today you're a university grad, surfing lines
of poetry, making waves, diving deep
into justice and equality issues.

In your scientific voice, you explain
the protoplasm of a living cell as it swims
under a microscope, or spotlight moths
late at night, documenting your findings
for posterity.

Now you lift me, your grandmother,
into the future, believing I'll always
be safe, never drown, splashing free
from prejudice, pollution, and violence.

the chameleon

Evelyn, my mom, writes lengthy poems
in birthday cards, sips Earl Grey tea,
reads tea-leaves predicting the arrival
of a letter. I believe her crimson geraniums
bloom because she talks to them. Not many
roll their own cigarettes but Mom's an expert—
smooth and straight as plastic straws.

I think my friends are oblivious to her loud
sudden outbursts … It's no secret.
Mom yells at clerks in the Co-op store,
returns food at restaurants
          (too hot or too cold)
and once, on a crisp autumn night, she left
the hospital in a gown and a cap of anger.

Sometimes, she's smooth silk.
Yes, Mom leaves me walking on wounded
feet, but I wish I'd saved her poems.

Helen E. Herr

I'm not like my mother

We have many questions as we consider
becoming foster parents. We invite a social
worker to visit our home in Turtleford.
She explains the joys and struggles
that often occur.

I'm a stay-at-home mom. We have a large home,
two children in school and one infant
at home. My husband
is willing to share this new responsibility.
We are approved and soon discover
it's not easy being a foster parent.

One summer day while walking a First Nations'
child in a stroller, I meet a senior from our
church. I joyfully say:

> *Meet our new wonderful baby boy.*

She replies:

> *Get him away from me.*
> *I don't want to see him!*

This is my first experience of prejudice,
but not my last.

it was in her eyes

Crystal, age two, is our first foster child,
and we jump at the chance to adopt her.
The name Crystal
was always a favourite,
so she keeps her birth name.

When my mother comes to visit,
she glances at our new daughter,
turns and looks the other way.
        Not a word. Not a hug.

How can my mother be so cruel?

Crystal, now in her fifties, tells me
she never forgot that moment.

        It was in her eyes!

Helen E. Herr

barn slowly disappears
two silver turrets
captains of the ship
last to slump
below the horizon

winter panics my skin

At the Calgary hospital, winter panics my skin.
Your legs, swollen telephone poles, unbendable
like your courage. Heart monitor beeps what's left
of your independence. Your milk-bone hands lay
in your lap. You, Kirby, so wanting to be well.

Visitors joke about your earlier days. There's no laughter
left in you. Dad arrives, takes your hand
and says: *I wish I could change places with you.*

> *It's okay, Dad, I've had a good run.*
> *I just want palliative care in my home.*

We take turns sitting beside your bed. It takes a long
time to say goodbye. Your sister, Shelley, tells stories
of your youth. Reads her poetry. We think you are
sleeping. When she goes to leave you say:

> *Aren't we going to play any more?*

not yoga

I lay on my back, eyes
closed, mouth closed.
My heels touch and my toes
point upward.

Legs, straight parallel bars,
bony knees touching,
my hands relax on my abdomen.
I deep-breathe in and out …
in and out ... in ... out ...
in … out …

When I open my eyes,
I find myself staring
at the ceiling.

You see, I'm practising
for palliative care.

*period at the end of the line**

The nurse whispers: *He's gone.* Our son
rests in his bed, too still, head turned, eyes
closed. His wife, Laurel, weeps quietly
beside him.

Our family enters, kneels and recites
The Lord's Prayer.
We each say good-bye.
Coffee is on but we have no taste
for conversation. Sadness is a heavy cloud.

A friend from the funeral home prepares
Kirby for transport through the garage,
past his golf cart.

Unseen, I slip away—remove the cloth
from his face and give him one last kiss
on the forehead.

---

*   (title from poem: Ellis Island #3, The Horse Knows the Way" by Dave Margoshes, used with permission.)

a pelican pause

Our family gathers at our cabin, circles the fire pit as Shelley plays
familiar tunes on a guitar. Few sing. Tomorrow Kirby's ashes
will be released into our favourite pond.
Heather arranges for a pontoon
to be docked for a morning boarding.

Our short cruise is smooth as we slip through tall reeds,
past campsites partly hidden by shoreline trees.
The motor is finally silenced.

Ron plays his Aboriginal flute
as Laurel tips the urn. Kirby's ashes
float among yellow water-lilies
then slowly sink.

Tissues pass between us.
Crystal hugs her two grandchildren,
too young to understand.

A great White American Pelican, black outer wing feathers
and huge orange bill, watches from the peak of a beaver den.
When the music stops, this colonial bird
gracefully lifts its twenty pounds, circles twice over the pontoon.
No one whispers as his wings tip a farewell before disappearing
over the Northern Boreal forest.[*]

---

[*]   Birds of Western Canada guidebook, page 98, 2013

Is this who I am?

Following our son's internment, I begin
a Spiritual Direction program, Benedictine
Monastery, Pecos, New Mexico, U.S.A.

With no Sunday classes, we are driven
to Santa Fe. Local women smile and visit
while sitting on their colourful hand-woven
carpets, selling souvenirs.

People gather in the park.
I toss crumbs to the pigeons and watch
an artist paint bold abstract art,
black background with purple splashes,
a red rose in the center.

When she notices my interest, she invites
me over. I ask:

> *What does the red rose mean?*
> She replies: *It's my heart*.

We talk. When it's time to leave, she says,

> *Helen, paint your feelings!*

Helen E. Herr

*how do I begin**

a new life in this
strange land
when I don't remember
where I began?

---

*   Tanka published in the 2019
     Haiku Canada Members' Anthology

be careful what you ask for

In my forties, I become restless.
I'm looking for answers to the question:
What am I to do the rest of my life?

In a time of silence, I hear my voice
give the answer—*go into ministry!*

You've got to be kidding. I'm shy,
have a family and never speak publically—
                (*but why do I feel so happy?*)

My family doesn't believe it.
My husband jokes—*Just a passing fad.*
Others say—*It must be a mid-life crisis!*

For me, there's no turning back.
Ordination comes seven years later.

the mystery

I'm excited when I receive the call from Edson, Alberta
to become their minister. The new church
has an active congregation, a great music ministry
and supportive people.
Everything fits.

> Into my second year, it's not working.
> I feel burdened as though I'm carrying
> a bag of stones.

My husband becomes estranged,
I'm homesick for family,
my health deteriorates.

Again, I ask the question—*What now God?*
A voice, other than my own, gives me a new name
and instruction to *study Cree.* I have no idea
the meaning of this message, but I feel a joy
that causes me to dance.

Filled with confidence, I resign.

missing link

I return home to Meadow Lake,
expect it to be quite some time
before I have an invitation
to consider ministry with First Nations.
Little do I know
Round Lake Pastoral charge, near Broadview,
is praying for a minister.

In less than two weeks, I'm on my way
to meet these people from two congregations.
I say *Yes* to the call.
Jim, soon to retire, will join me.

Our children have left home for careers.
I just begin mine.

one mistake and then another

I gown in my white ordination alb
for Sunday worship on the reserve
until one day a woman from our church
says: *You don't have to wear that,*
        we know who you are.

Once, I bring an advent wreath to church
and light a candle every Sunday until I learn
through the grapevine:

        Lighting candles reminds
        us of residential school.

It's a learning curve down.
Every false step, a tedious
climb back to acceptance.

helter-skelter

I'm blind as I begin native ministry,
have no knowledge of First Nations' faith
or life experience.

When a woman in the congregation approaches
me at church, tears mist her eyes:

> *My husband is terrified,*
> *under the curse.*
> *Please come.*

This is unfamiliar territory.
I pray: *Bless this home, bind*
and cast out the spirit of fear.
I mark every doorway
with the sign of the cross.

The family holds hands around the kitchen
table. A daughter, age five, prays:

> *Make my daddy well.*

The cattle run helter-skelter, I'm told.
A sign prayers are answered.

Helen E. Herr

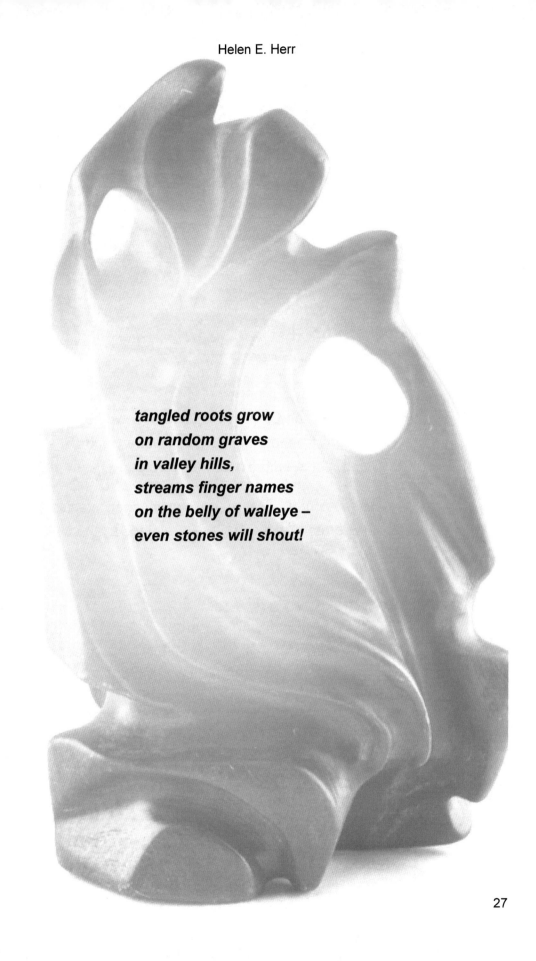

tangled roots grow
on random graves
in valley hills,
streams finger names
on the belly of walleye –
even stones will shout!

The following Cree naming has been written in the "y" dialect from the *Plains Cree Dictionary* and *Let's Learn Cree*, edited by Anne Anderson.

My apologies for any Cree spelling inaccuracies in **Stones Will Shout**; they are made by the author.

Helen E. Herr

sekisewin[*]

Iskwewak march, holding banners:

> *stop infant deaths,*
> *poverty, suicide, addictions,*
> *abuse, missing women!*

Under crows' fanned wings
of night, abducted *Iskwewak*
have no place to run,
no cave in which to hide.
Their screams are heard
only by seagulls lifting
in unison from Crooked Lake,
terrified of silent voices
screaming Cree.

---

[*]   sekisiwin – fear
       iskwewak - women

*pipon**

In the rear-view mirror
I see you stagger,
fall in the ditch.
My driver will not stop.

In the news:

> *Aboriginal hit and killed*
> *on Highway Number One*
> *east of Regina.*

No one knows
we once joined hands
in a prayer circle
in your living room,
you prayed for me.

---

*   *pipon* = winter

Helen E. Herr

pimpahtaw mistatim[*]

He's chopping wood
in his yard, stacking
winter's supply
for his home in the valley.

From a distance,
I tell him who I am.

*I know who you are,
          I don't want to talk to you.*

With each swing of the axe—
sharp, ear-splitting curses.

Back on the road,
I dig splinters
out of my skin.

---

[*]   pimpahtaw mistatim = running horse

sestuk*

Jacob Bear United Church
women meet once a week,
bring their knitting needles.
Between stitches,
they share everyday events:
a daughter's wedding,
the birth of a child,
a cousin's disappearance.

> *Will my grandchild come home*
> *from the city in a box?*

One elder's arthritic hands,
gnarled as a tree,
knits for children in the north.

> *Your socks don't match,* I say.

> *No, even unmatched socks*
> *keep your feet warm,* she replies.

---

*   sestuk = yarn

Helen E. Herr

apukoses[*]

Wednesday evening Bible study
in the church basement.
Sheets of prepared notes
on the Matthew text are given
to each person.
No-one speaks.
What's wrong?
I stumble over my words.

Everyone bursts with laughter:

> *There's a mouse watching*
> *from the corner of the room.*

I laugh, just to make it look
as though I really don't mind.
But, if the ladies look under
the table, they'll see
my feet held high.

---

[*]   apukoses = mouse

wapiski oohoo[*]

As I visit a patient
in a Regina hospital,
two RCMP officers
escort a man in shackles.
His mother is ill.

As he holds her hand,
my eyes are fixed on the metal
wrist and leg bands.

An elder speaks to me:

Look outside the window.

> *A white owl will not leave*
> *until the sick person dies.*

---

[*]   *wapiski oohoo* = white owl

Helen E. Herr

atimosis[*]

Six-year-old laughter, climber
of fences, trees, and trucks
until one day …
you and friends play
   I'm the king of the castle
on a power transformer
in Regina.

I'm voiceless as I stand gowned
in white beside your hospital bed.

   Only five minutes, the nurse says,
   fourth degree burns.

Seven friends circle
your coffin—
hold hands, talk
about riding bikes with you.

_____

*   atimosis = puppy

*kahkakiw**

Into the hills,
strong backs carry the casket
past a chief's grave, long collapsed
inside a picket fence.

Young men take turns
filling this latest grave,
mound made smooth
as wind-washed stone
then showered with flowers.

We sit on blankets
near the unnamed white crosses,
eat soup and chicken,
drink hot tea,
tell stories, laugh a lot.

---

*   kahkakiw = raven

Helen E. Herr

*oskusakiy**

Taxis come to the church
the day the used clothing truck arrives.
I feel itchy as I watch
from the sidelines.

Women burrow through fabric,
jackets, shirts, dresses, pants.
They layer their arms with treasures,
hide them from my view
and wear them on Sunday.

Years later,
a business woman comments:

I like your coat – is it new?

Yes, I reply,
I bought it at the thrift store.

---

*   oskusakiy - new skin

pesim[*]

Everyone in town knows Mr. Crow.
You'll find him in the cafe or walking
the streets, or he may appear
at funeral lunches for a bite to eat.

Once in a while, Mr. Crow knocks
on my door, stands in the porch.
I invite him for coffee but he always says no.

He quotes Bible stories,
knows them well. We pray together,
then he leaves.

I remember one Sunday, Mr. Crow
stood at the back of the church.
Watched me raise my arms in a blessing—
then I watch him raise his arms,
blessing me.

---

*   pesim - the sun

Helen E. Herr

wapimusk[*]

There are no phone calls
or invitations to tell me I'm wanted.
My First Nations' friends welcome me
in other ways:

A *Kohkom* wings her arms
around my shoulders—

> *I give big bear hugs,* she says.
> (her name is Bear)

An artist opens his door and speaks:

Why did you take so long to get here?

Holding hands, we all dance
a Round dance on Veterans' Day.
Prayers are said.

Now I treasure those moments,
warmed by gifts of blankets
at pow-wows and my farewell.
What greater love than this?

Why did I leave?

---

[*]   wapimusk - polar bear
       kohkom - grandmother

Plough wind oscillates
the lofty pine,
branches plead insanity,
beg Ezekiel's breath
give life to dry bones,*

before the trunk crumbles
into sticks
that light the night
with crackling.

---

*   Ezekiel 37:7

Helen E. Herr

little do they know

Ron, often called Bear, busks near
the South Saskatchewan River
on Spadina Crescent in Saskatoon.

In his sun-yellow shirt with rainbow
ribbons, he plays original melodies
on his hand-carved flute.

Few stop to listen, not many
even give him a glance.
No time for pan-handlers.
No time for Bear.

Little do others know he's travelled
the world, danced the Sun Dance,
spoken at international conferences.
This pipe-carrier, elder, story-teller,
plays melodies that make seniors
tap their feet and children giggle.

Stop and listen—
        you'll discover who you are.

not a nursery rhyme

Peppered with rage, painter
squeezes blobs of blue
and geranium-red oil paint
into a metal tray. Fingered
in latex gloves, he wildly rolls
walls, spatters windows
and clothes, drips purple puddles
in front of the refrigerator.
Footprints mix bread crumbs
and paint as he circles the room.

*fast pedaling**

Faster than runners
race to the end of days
flee nightmares
chase daydreams
spin in circles
in the black of night
howl at the moon
until someone hears
his voice.

---

*   *#6, eight night poems, Transition Magazine 2010, revised

masks

1.

> *McDonalds cafeteria in Wal-Mart,*
> *October 31st, after sundown.*

One woman, six foot tall, wears a flaming silk dress
covered with cut-out paper leaves.
She's a stiff autumn tree leaning against the wall,
glaring at my chocolate milkshake.
A man in black stares at me
through his mask … an aging Spider-Man?

I grab my milkshake and leave
to drive a friend to a pawn shop—
a first for me.

The room's like an old warehouse—
huge, dusty and musty.

> Pain crawls walls:
> castaway electronics, out-of-tune instruments,
> leather jackets with tattered fringes.
> Limp jingle dresses dangle from the ceiling.
>
> Under glass, engagement rings hide—
> tarnished and ashamed.

(masks continued)

2.

Bear screams at the clerks: *You put grease on my*
white leather pow-wow outfit! It cost me one thousand
dollars! I covered it with plastic and look what you did,
you ...!
His curses would frighten ghosts.
Clerks remain stone-faced.

Rushing through the exit, Bear bumps
his claimed treasures against the door frame:

> two flutes, one guitar in its original box,
> his soiled outfit.

Outside, he wears the mask of a raging lion,
kick-boxes bricks on the east side of the building
with such force I fear he'll break his foot.

In the car, my legs shake like leaves
in a hailstorm.
Bear ignores my no smoking sign.
My face: a chalk-white mask.

wanting

I sprinkle water from a bottle—
                as if the water is holy—
on the ground beneath the tree
with the broken branch.

Your frayed belt
is given to the paramedic at the hospital.

One month later,
I meet Bear for coffee in a restaurant
at the same corner where he plays
his flute and collects coins.

We exchange gifts.
Forgiveness.

Helen E. Herr

standing in the shadows

The fringe on her powwow shawl
flutters above rose-beaded
moccasins. She smoothes the coloured
ribbons on her shirt, hand-stitched
by her father, Ron, who lives in Canada.

He remembers the Sun Dance:
   searing heat, no water allowed,
   hooks tearing chest and back,
   promises given, then broken—
reason enough to stand in shadows.

Kyara dances the Jingle Dance for him.
Rubs her ribbons between two fingers,
swirls away her father's sadness.
If she dances quickly, the sunshine ribbons
will circle him, turn his brown shirt yellow—
perfect for his next dance.

the flute is silenced

Early morning, the doctor phones
from the hospital: staff found Ron dead
and they couldn't revive him.

Suicide.

Ron told me he wanted to walk
into the light, and now he has.

——————

The band hall is packed.
Sage smokes around our feet
as we view Ron laid out
on white silk in an oak casket.

Everyone touches his cold body.
Drums beat. Singers stretch their voices.
Crystal tucks cigarettes into Ron's pocket,
another person places a sweetgrass braid
and tobacco into his hands.

I join many speakers to honour him.
Our family is invited to sit behind the casket
with his Cree relatives. All of the band members
file past, shake our hands, give
us a hug—and often a kiss on the cheek.

We feel welcomed as family.

Helen E. Herr

square tires

Car lights pierce the ink of night.
Thirty-five degrees below zero. Square tires
thump as we crawl towards the cemetery.
White wooden crosses staccato the hillside.

Your coffin, covered with brightly-patterned
Native blankets, is lowered into the rough box.

A hammer cracks frost, seals the lid.
The backhoe is waiting. It chugs
into position, fills your grave, drags earth
and snow as it shapes a mound
for layering blankets and flowers.

Silence.

No drums, pipes or voices—
only footsteps crunching snow
as we circle your grave,
then leave death behind.

At the hall, lunch is ready. Hot soup
tastes excellent until someone tells me
I'm eating moose-eye soup.

All smile for family photos.

frozen

Men gather on the other side of the tracks,
scathed by time, drugs, gambling
and other habits that demolish lives.

They collect empties, sell them and toss
the day's earnings into a common pot.
Whoever is sober buys cheap wine
at the corner liquor board store.

In cold weather, they sleep in the shelter—

> breakfast and coffee
> clean socks, toques and mitts—
> before they're sent into the streets.

Their footsteps kick up the snow.

From his sidewalk hangout, protected
from wind, a guitar player
waves to his buddy.
A passerby offers him money for coffee.

> *Thanks for the money, but I'll share it*
> *with my friends.*

four smooth creases

Since World War II, a mother
understands her son suffers
from Post-Traumatic Stress Syndrome.

She searches for him.

The blizzard howls through the night.
A police woman knocks on her door.
Hands her an envelope:

> *Sorry, we haven't found your son.*
> *He's now listed as a missing person.*

The mother thanks her for searching,
closes the door and folds the crisp
white paper into four smooth creases—
slips it beside the crucified
in the family Bible.

humus

Veterans fall one by one,
officials lay wreaths.
Poppies cling to boot tops
of a bronzed unknown soldier.

Adults hush babies with soothers,
grasp hands of toddlers.
Last post demands silence.

A black crow listens
from a telephone wire,
cocks his head left, right,
squawks his own Reveille.

oil flows over your face
seeps through grooves
peeks into holes
until your brown belly
shines

in the eyes of the loon

Smoke from Western Canadian
forest fires halos the Swiss sun.
Daughter drapes a cherry-red shawl
around her shoulders.

The wind flutters her fringe
and waves her tangerine skirts
through lakes and rivers—seen
only in the eyes of the loon.

On a Saskatchewan beach,
an artist brushes magenta
onto canvas—
oblivious of moose fleeing south
in search of blueberries.

Helen E. Herr

on the edge

Shaking winter's cold,
sunrise sheds
tangerine streaks
in the distance.
Crocuses, first to bloom,
dress frosty hills
in mauve.

Mesmerized
by ice crystals
chiming on the river,
duck totters
on the edge—
watches drake
swimming in the clouds,
risks the dive.

kinship

At our cabin at Greig Lake
in northern Saskatchewan,
a neighbourhood deer ambles
into the yard. Dust twirls around
her ankles, socks grey and white—
zebra stripes.

I extend a green bouquet of grass
from the base of our birch trees.
Missy swirls it around her mouth
as a cow would chew its cud.

My camera clicks … clicks.
The doe leaves wet droplets
on the lens, moves on
to the neighbour's box of grain, hidden
under sweeping pine branches.

Today the box is empty.
A new bylaw is posted at the store:
"Feeding wild animals in the park
is against the law."

Missy can't read.

Helen E. Herr

transparent in the laundromat

Two women washing clothes at the lake's laundromat:

> one woman takes a damp cloth,
> wipes the washer clean,
> polishes the communal table—
> spotless.

By nine a.m.:
> her make-up's in place,
> yellow shorts ironed,
> hair in organized twists.

I wear flip-flops,
wind combs my hair.
I toss clothes into the machine,
> never check it for cleanliness—
> never even consider it.

Who is this woman who refuses to look at me?

I would love to lead her to my campsite,
watch her crawl out of the tent, after the rain—
with three children and a dog.*

---

*   The Society, page 24, 2015, revised.

it must have been the cashews

My clothes stick—no sunscreen,
no sunglasses.

Plunked onto the sand,
forty degree heat, sinking fingers
into a brown paper bag—
                    cashews.
Salt-licking good.

Waves summersault—
                    strings of pearls worn by Irish dancers
kicking heel-toe-polkas.

My eyes blur ... gulls become poems
in foreign languages.

A stranger helps me up the hill to the store
for anything cold.

> *Please, a double-decker*
> *tiger-tiger waddle cone.*
> *I mean waffle cone, with tiger drips,*
> *no, no... a chocolate peas, please.*

Are you okay? the clerk asks.

No thanks, I reply,
I'm fastidious!

Helen E. Herr

bank corners in the wind

Seagulls posture on one leg,
single file along the shore
seeking morning flying orders—
      some are directed to guard
      buoys, others map routes
      in the sand. Fledglings
      still learning to bank corners
      in the wind.

In the evening, nine seagulls
and one lost duck
park and face west
on the slippery dock.

Emily Carr country

I do enjoy Saskatchewan summers
but in winter, I fly west
to visit Vancouver Island.

I burrow beneath feathered duvets
in a cedar lodge.

> I become a tree,
> feet in the soil,
> arms reaching—
>   a dream catcher
> rooted in history.

> Pine becomes
> my essential oil,

> rain—

>   my sleeping pill.

pretzels

West coast storm
blasts beaches, logs
twist into pretzels,
wave before drowning.

Centurion stump,
half-smothered in sand,
balances a beer mug.

Black-eyed oak refuses
to face the ocean,
ashamed to be a bench
on the beach.

exposure

Sunshine cracks darkness
where shadows hide
under ferns and palms.

Arbutus limbs blush
at their nakedness.
Ocean drenches
hashbrown-and-white speckled stones,
chases night storms away.

Helen E. Herr

exquisite soapstone
I shape your wings
with green feathers
so you may journey
to your new home

today I put my babies to bed

Soapstone babies
in my hands for one year—
soon to become confused teens—

broken
ashamed
misunderstood.

Hiding in garage boxes
or sleeping in the car's trunk—

waiting
to be discovered.

Helen E. Herr

crow's feet walking

When people learn
we've been married for sixty-two years
some say: *You deserve a medal.*

Perhaps, but years do take their toll:
children, grief, stress, and boredom
undoubtedly affect my outward appearance:

> lines around the mouth,
> wrinkles at the corner of my eyes—
> *crow's feet* they're called.

Yet others say: *You look young for your age.*

I'll tell you my secret—
> I practice smiling, daily.

folded neatly under blankets

This is the day to tidy my linen closet.

Blankets, sheets, pillow-cases, towels
and a parcel wrapped in white tissue—

    my mother's hand-crocheted tablecloth, forever stained—

all tumble to the floor.

I bag everything, toss it into the Diabetes recycle bin
at the edge of town.

I remember Mom's quick-wristed crocheting
as she sat in her straight-backed hostess chair,
pastel-flowered dress draped
below her knees, ankles crossed,
three-inch heels.

Now I wish I could cradle her handiwork
across my knee—
        pretend I know how to crochet.

Set Mother free
from small, perfect stitches.

rubbish

It's hard to watch friends balance the piano
over the deck railing, turn the corner
to our second floor condo.

People say: *No more moves!*
They talk in coffee shops
about all Jim's stuff—

> retired golf clubs, Christmas
> lights, tools never used,
> broken bicycle parts,
> high chair and stroller,
> boxes of dolls,
> and flea market surprises

saved for grandchildren

who'll never use them.

This dust and disorder leaves me
no place to hide.

Black tornado nightmares
sweep me out the window
onto his heap of junk
on the lawn.

He calls them treasures.
I call them by another name.

the tenth day

Watercolour paper wedged
beneath a double bed.

Dry paint brushes,
nestled in rolls of rainbow cotton,
hide beneath panties
in the sock drawer.

Empty frames dangle
from curtain rods;
colour wheels mix
in my dreams.

Blank Arches paper buried
in boxes and stacked beneath
last winter's coats.

My art studio lacks walls.
Since moving day—
            nothing has a home.

misfit

I'm a poor fit for condo living.
Doors open-close; I wonder who?

Car doors slam.
I hear footsteps in the hall
and begin to shake.

Birds enjoy condo living:

> perch on high poles away from cats,
> gossip on fences,
> nest at sunset.
> fly south when weather chills,
> return in spring.

They always belong.

shredded

Today, my children move me
to the care home.
They sort my life:

> three packed boxes for family,
> > another for the garbage,
> the rest for auction.

I beg family to save my treasured box
stored under the bed:

> selected cards from friends,
> obituaries, a faded rose
> > from my first love,
> mother's linen hanky with pink roses
> > and crocheted ochre edging.

> Already gone.

Helen E. Herr

twilight haven

I'm welcomed, ushered down the halls:

> *This is your room, number nineteen.*
> *To the right is your bath.*
> > *(Only go there with a nurse)*

> *No nail holes on these freshly-painted walls,*
> *and this bulletin board is for posting meals, only.*

> *(Where can I put my family photos?)*

> *I'll come and get you for meals.*

cornflakes taste like grass

I share meals with Susan.
Size Two, whimsical net-wrapped hair
and she continually mutters:

> *All I want to do is help somebody…*
> *all I want to do is help somebody…*

The kitchen is off-limits.

> (I could at least stir cookie dough!)

What is there for me to do here?
Many tasks are fulfilled by the housekeeping staff
who leave wrinkles in my bed
and flies on the windowsill.

> (I must remember to ask for a fly-swatter)

I'm useless without my albums.
Can't match time and place.
Faces blur, names are lost.

In this house, seasons never change.

Helen E. Herr

bloomers

It's spring. I miss my garden.

If you want flowers, you have
to paint them, I'm told.

I whirl the brush upward
and green rabbit ears appear.
I dab tulips—orange as my teapot—
and they make me laugh.

Quick delicate brushstrokes
for white-bonnet flowers with purple-
fluted edges. They hide beneath
leaves. Only I can find them!

On unbalanced days, I paint blue
stems dripping from the ceiling.
Yellow daisies with black eyes
sweep the dust-covered floor—
        I feel better just looking at them.

Not many know about my garden.
I'll show you if you like.

Meet The Author

Helen Erlene (Greer) Herr is the second in a line of four female writers. As a mother of five and foster parent to twenty-five, her life has been shaped by the children and adults who surround her. ***Stones Will Shout*** is Helen's first published book. She hopes readers will read her poems slowly, and connect to them with their personal and collective stories.

Helen has enjoyed each phase of her life. She's been a registered piano teacher (ARCT); a United Church organist; obtained her Master of Divinity from St. Andrew's College in Saskatoon; and was ordained in the United Church of Canada.

Upon retirement, Helen completed the University of Saskatchewan Art and Design Certificate program, with a major in Soapstone.

Helen lives in Watrous, SK. She participates in her church and community through Blue Sky Writers'; Saskatchewan Writers Guild programs; Spirit of Manitou Studio Trail; Gallery on 3rd in Watrous; and juried art shows.

Printed in Canada